Science Technology Engineering Math

STEM STARTERS FOR KIDS

BOTANY

ACTIVITY

Book

Packed with Activities
and Botany Facts!

Written by Jenny Jacoby

Designed and illustrated
by Vicky Barker

FOR
YOUNG
READERS

10 9 8 7 6 5 4 3 2 1

Text by Jenny Jacoby
Design by Vicky Barker

ISBN
978-1-63158-694-1

Printed in China

WHAT IS BOTANY?

Botany is a part of biology, which is the study of all living things. Botany is all about plants: their structure, where they live, how they grow and spread, and how they interact with the world, including humans and other animals. Plants are so important to people and all living things, and they help the world look the way it does. Studying plants helps us to understand more about them and how we can look after them and protect our world for everyone.

WHAT IS STEM?

STEM stands for "science, technology, engineering, and mathematics." These four areas are closely linked, and can be used to study and make sense of everything around us—which includes plants. By understanding plants and the things they need, we will be better at protecting them—which helps to keep everything on the planet happy and healthy! Together, STEM can help find problems, solve problems, and improve our lives in ways nobody has even thought of yet!

Science

Technology

Engineering

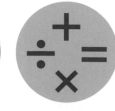
Math

WHAT IS A PLANT?

If you imagine a plant, what do you see? It probably has green leaves, a stem, perhaps a colorful flower, and sits in the ground. That is what most plants do look like and each of these features does an important job to keep the plant alive and growing.

There are also plants that live in water, and plants that have no flowers or even roots. Some plants keep their stems underground while other plants have stems (or trunks) so huge they can grow taller than Big Ben!

All plants are:
- Alive
- Green (almost always)
- Able to make their own food
- Made up of a substance called cellulose

What aren't plants?
Mushrooms and other fungi are not plants. Plants make their own food from air and water, but fungi get their food from their environment. Some do this by growing on dead plants and animals, and by taking their nutrients they help to decompose their bodies.

Flower
where seeds are made, so new plants can grow

Stem
delivers water and nutrients around the plant

Leaves
where food is made

Roots
keep the plant steady in the ground, and absorb water and nutrients

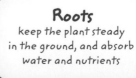

Plants come in all
shapes and sizes and
are everywhere!
In this city scene,
look out for:

- Grass
- A spiky cactus
- 5 tall trees
- 6 red flowers
- 8 yellow flowers
- Moss
- Lichen (on trees)
- A tree with a very
  wide trunk
- A bush with lots of
  purple flowers
- Pondweed
- Water lilies
- A log

Answers on page 30.

LOOKING AT PLANTS

Botanists are plant scientists. Botanists study plants using many of the same skills that all scientists use.

Observation

All science begins with observation—looking carefully and making notes. What is special about this plant?

Ideas and questions

Observing things is a good way of coming up with ideas. You observe that this plant has leaves with two different colors—what questions does this make you think of?

Testing

You've asked some questions, so now you need to do some tests to find out the answers. To test if leaves with two different colors behave differently from green leaves, you would do the same test on the two different plants and compare the results.

Classifying

Botanists use the information they have found out to classify plants into different groups—a bit like a family tree. Plants are grouped with others that share similar appearances or that work in similar ways.

Why might that be?

Do they act differently from leaves that are all green?

How does it happen?

Are the leaves good to eat or poisonous?

Botanists also use some special tools.

Test your observation skills by finding ten differences between these two plant scenes. Answers on page 30.

Potometer

This measures how much water transpires through the plant and into the air in a given time.

Microscope

To look at the tiny structures inside plants.

Pocket magnifying glass

To look closely at growing plants without cutting them.

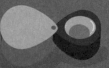

Fast Green

A chemical that dyes plant cells so they're easier to see under a microscope.

HOW PLANTS DRINK

Just like us, plants need water to live. Without enough to drink they go floppy, shrivel up, and die. Plants "drinking" is called **transpiration.**

Plants take in water from the soil through their roots. It travels up through tubes in the stem or trunk, like a straw. The water finally exits the plant through holes in the leaves called **stomata** ,individually called a **stoma.** It exits as an invisible gas called water vapor.

Water keeps the plant's cells **turgid** (full of water) so that they are strong enough to support the plant.

Water is needed by the leaves so they can make food. This process is called **photosynthesis**.

Water brings nutrients from the soil with it, which the plant needs to grow. We can help plants by adding nutrient-rich compost or fertilizer to the soil.

Water enters the roots when needed by the plant. In hot or windy weather, plants transpire more quickly because the heat and wind encourage the water to escape the leaves more quickly. If there's not much water available at the roots, leaves close their stomata to stop the water leaving the plant, which slows down transpiration.

Color in these parts
that are important in
transpiration.

Water = blue
Stomata = green
Sunshine = yellow
Nutrients = brown

Stoma
open

Stoma
closed

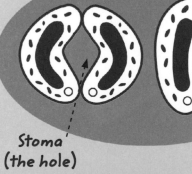

Stoma
(the hole)

Answers on
page 30.

9

PHOTOSYNTHESIS

Photosynthesis is a special chemical reaction that plants use to make food for themselves. It means "putting together with light" because sunlight provides the energy the plant needs to put together simple chemicals to make food.

The reaction happens inside the cells of green leaves. Leaves are green because they are full of **chlorophyll,** which is the chemical that helps absorb energy from the sunshine for photosynthesis to happen.

The other chemicals come from the air and soil. Carbon dioxide in the air enters the leaves through stomata, and water travels up from the roots to the leaves.

Glucose is a sugary carbohydrate that the plant uses for food—and animals do too, when they eat plants!

Oxygen is a waste product and it leaves the plant through the stomata.

The chlorophyll does its job inside tiny structures in the plant cells called chloroplasts.

Carbon dioxide

Chloroplast

Cell wall

Vacuole

Nucleus

Water

Help this plant to
photosynthesize by drawing
in what it needs:

Sunlight
Green leaves
Water

Carbon dioxide

PROPAGATION

Propagation is the way plants make more plants, like having plant children. They do this in two main ways. Some plants need two parents to make a new plant—this is called **sexual reproduction.** Pollen from one parent meets the ovule of the second parent when a flower is pollinated. Other plants are able to make identical copies of themselves without needing another plant—this is called **asexual reproduction.**

Both types of reproduction work well but both have benefits and costs.

	Sexual	Asexual
What's the benefit?	Each new plant has a mixture of characteristics from both of its parents, so has a chance to be a better version of its parents.	It's quicker—plants can make copies of themselves whenever they need to.
What's the cost?	Plants rely on other things (such as wind, water, animals and insects) to bring seeds to them, so they can't control when propagation will happen.	Each "child" plant is identical to its parent, so it will inherit all its bad characteristics as well as its good ones.

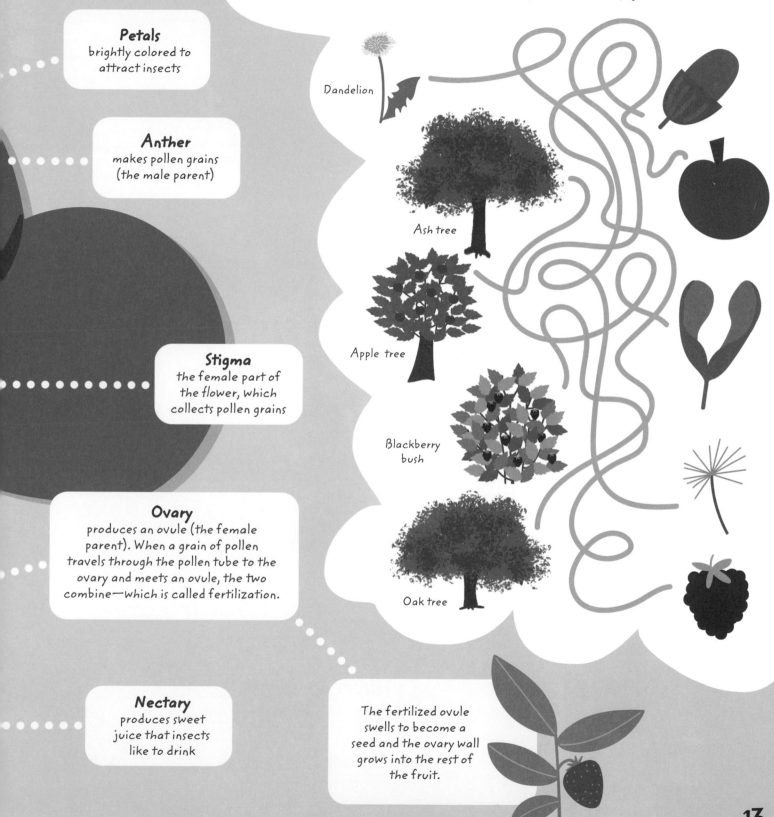

Petals
brightly colored to attract insects

Anther
makes pollen grains (the male parent)

Stigma
the female part of the flower, which collects pollen grains

Ovary
produces an ovule (the female parent). When a grain of pollen travels through the pollen tube to the ovary and meets an ovule, the two combine—which is called fertilization.

Nectary
produces sweet juice that insects like to drink

Different plants use different ways to spread their seeds. Follow the lines to find out which seed comes from which plant. Answers on page 30.

Dandelion

Ash tree

Apple tree

Blackberry bush

Oak tree

The fertilized ovule swells to become a seed and the ovary wall grows into the rest of the fruit.

HABITATS

Plants come in all different sizes and styles, each suited to its natural habitat—the place where it grows best. Plants that grow where there's not much rain are adapted to hold on to as much water as possible. Plants that grow where there are four different seasons in the year are adapted to change with the seasons. Whatever the environment, there will (probably) be a plant adapted to live there!

In the **rainforest**, plants are adapted to cope with shallow soil and lots of heavy rain. Trees have thick buttresses to keep them steady, thin bark to help water evaporate and pointy leaves to help the water drip off.

Where there are **four seasons** in a year, trees produce lots of leaves in the summer to make the most of the sunny season and lose their leaves in winter to save energy in cold weather.

In the **desert**, plants have thick, waxy leaves to keep water in and long roots to absorb as much water as possible when it does rain.

Rainforest

Deciduous forest

Desert

PLANTS AND PEOPLE

People need plants—we couldn't survive without them! We help each other in so many ways. When people understand the good that plants do, they look after plants and grow more of them.

Cleaning air and water

As well as removing carbon dioxide, plants also remove toxins from the air. Water plants can help filter dirty water so that it becomes safe to drink and for other animals to live in.

Food

Plants use the energy from the Sun to create food. When we eat plants, we eat that energy—so plants help us take energy from the Sun too!

Materials

We use plant materials for all sorts of things—from paper for books and writing to timber for buildings. Humans aren't the only animals who rely on plants for making their homes. Beavers, birds, chimpanzees, and many more, take parts of plants and use them as building materials. Then there are all the animals and insects that make their homes in trees and plants, too.

Carbon store

Because plants turn carbon dioxide into energy they use for growing, they contain a lot of carbon. Human activity puts so much carbon dioxide into the air that it is causing global warming. Because plants capture carbon dioxide from the air and store it inside themselves, they are a big help in the fight against climate change.

Oxygen

People—and all animals—need oxygen to live. Our bodies use oxygen from the air we breathe, and we breathe out carbon dioxide. Plants need carbon dioxide to live, and they breathe out oxygen. This partnership means animals and plants depend on each other.

Tree bathing

Plants make us feel better and happier. Indoor plants can help us to concentrate and feel less stressed. Outside, "forest bathing" helps us to feel calm and happy, too.

Write down or draw your five favorite things about plants. If you are writing with a pencil, you might even be using a plant product now!

FROM ROCKS TO FOREST

Not all plants can just start growing wherever their seeds land. Some need other plants around to shelter them from strong weather. Others can start growing almost anywhere! These are called **pioneer species** because they can turn barren, empty land into places where other plants can grow.

No flowers: seeds are wind-pollinated as few insects visit barren land

Green for photosynthesising their own food

Reproduce asexually to make it easier and quicker to spread

1. On rocky land, where there is no soil, only hardy, small plants like lichen and moss can grow. You might notice this on bricks and walls near your home.

2. When the pioneer species dies, fungi, and bacteria help to break it down into leaf mould. This is like soil, and it is full of nutrients so other small plants can begin to grow in it.

3. New plants that grow are called **secondary succession**.

4. Bigger plants that need stable places can now grow, until eventually the area turns into a forest.

Over a long time, this land has grown into a thick forest. Find your way through the forest to the other side—but don't trip on any roots!

START HERE

Answers on page 31.

HOW PLANTS IMPROVE PLACES

All over the world are places that can be improved by plants.
They not only help the landscape but also help the people there.

The **Great Green Wall** is a huge project to plant a wall of trees across Africa. The "wall" will be made up of 11 million trees, across eleven countries and will be 5,000 miles long! The drought-resistant acacia trees will help stop the landscape turning to desert because of climate change.

In the desert

- Wind blows away the soil
- People need to water the ground
- Water evaporates easily
- There are no jobs for people to do

Where trees are planted

- Trees protect the soil and keep it in place
- Tree roots hold water in the soil—helping to fill up wells with water for people to drink
- The leaves make compost for the soil
- The canopy keeps the air humid and shady—so less watering is needed
- With more water available, it's easier to grow vegetables
- People can earn money from planting the trees and vegetables

Mangroves are tropical trees that like to grow in or near water, so they are perfectly suited to grow at the coast where the tide comes in and out. They are a natural way of protecting the land against powerful tropical storms, which can damage and wear away coastal areas.

- The tangle of roots in the water absorbs some of the power of the water in a storm surge—making the waves less dangerous on the land.
- The mangrove environment is home to all sorts of animals including tigers and dolphins, and fish and seafood for people and other animals to eat.
- The plants filter water coming from inland, removing pollution before it flows into the sea.

Make this mangrove forest look even healthier by drawing in some animals you might find there:
Tiger
Dolphins
Bees
Fish
Crabs
Birds
Monkeys

FARMING

For thousands of years, people have been planting seeds and helping plants to grow so they can harvest them and turn them into food. Today, we farm grains, pulses, fruit, and vegetables—and all these delicious foods start with a seed being planted in the ground.

Each year, farmers choose the best plants from each harvest to create the next year's seeds. On a year without much rain, for example, the plants that survive and grow will be the ones with a natural ability to cope with little water. Because the next year's seeds grow from these survivors, all their future plants will have the same ability to grow well in dry conditions.

This is how farmers help their crops adapt to their environment. Plants do it naturally, but farmers give them a helping hand.

Can you find these botany words in this word search?
Words can read backwards, forwards, up, down and diagonally.

```
d t h j d e l q s x y d e o h v p
y o v e g e t a b l e s g i u v e
k t i t t a s k u s e d i n e n a
c g d k s r u s l a d a p t a c t
a r e o a e i t o d a a e i r t u
b a a i r x v o u s t h s i t h t
d i s y d l t r m s v e e l f e a
e n w g r e m r a f d p e m v a i
e s v x a g o e r h d n d u o r l
f e s r c t p e s l n v s s l t p
h l t d h c v i o g f i e l d s o
i e p l r g r p m m p n g l r t f
c r o p r o c k s t x w n e n l e
d s y i s y u d s z e a a i o u r
a f r u i t e g s a m g o t e y c
s e l e e s i c h e x e c s e k j
g t a e h w y s e t j a v t f r a
```

adapt

drought

farmer

fields

grains

harvest

seeds

vegetables

water

wheat

crop

fruit

Answers on page 32.

EATING PLANTS

Because plants can turn sunlight, air, and water into food, they are called **producers**—they produce food from out of thin air! Animals can't do this, which is why animals need to eat plants or other animals for food.

During the growing season, plants make so much food that they store it by growing new bits (such as fruit, vegetables, or leaves) that can be nutritious and delicious for us to eat. Plants don't do this as a gift for us but because when we eat them we also help them to propagate. Imagine a bird eating a blackberry—when it poos out the undigested seeds, the seeds land on the ground with their own supply of fertilizer (the bird's poo). The bird has helped a new plant to grow, far from its parent where it won't compete with the parent for sunlight or nutrients.

Different edible plants are full of different nutrients that we need in our diet. By eating lots of different fruits, vegetables, and grains we can make sure to eat a healthy diet.

Draw more foods of each color in each section to create a rainbow of food.

 Tomatoes are full of vitamins A, C, and E, and potassium.

 Oranges are great for vitamin C, which keeps skin and bones healthy and helps wounds heal.

 Plantain contain antioxidants, which protect our cells and help keep the sugars balanced in our blood.

 Peas give us minerals such as phosphorus, magnesium, iron, zinc, and copper, which help us grow bones and blood cells, use our muscles and fight off infection.

 Blueberries contain vitamins and antioxidants, which protect our cells.

 Figs are rich in manganese, which helps our bodies build bones.

 Red cabbage is full of vitamins.

 Walnuts are rich in omega-3 fats, which keep our heart and blood healthy.

 Chia seeds are tiny but full of fibre, protein, and vitamins.

 Cauliflower has lots of vitamin C and helps to protect our cells from damage.

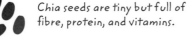

PLANTS FOR MEDICINE

Many plants have healing powers that people have used as medicine for thousands of years. Today, even some of the medicines made in laboratories and prescribed by doctors use chemicals taken from plants.

Ginger is good for helping to stop you feeling sick. You can eat it as food or drink it in hot water like a tea.

Aloe vera is a succulent plant with a thick gel inside its leaves, which is very soothing for the skin, helping it to heal itself. It's good to rub on sunburn straight from the plant, but aloe vera extract is also used in ointments and creams you can buy in shops.

Chilli peppers make your mouth feel hot when eaten, but when used in an ointment it can help to treat arthritis.

The **opium poppy** is used in laboratories to make a powerful painkiller called morphine, which is used in hospitals.

Yew trees are poisonous but the needles and bark are used in two powerful medicines to fight cancer. Both of these drugs are now made in a laboratory—but this is only now possible because scientists learned from Native Americans that the tree was good for fighting cancer.

Decorate these medicine bottles on the laboratory shelf. Design a label that tells the patient what each medicine will do.

GINGER

ALOE VERA

CHILLI PEPPERS

OPIUM POPPY

YEW TREES

RECORD-BREAKING PLANTS

Some plants are truly amazing. Here are some record-breakers.

The **tallest** tree in the world is a sequoia tree in California, named Hyperion. It is 379.7 feet tall!

The **smelliest** plant in the world is called the corpse flower because when the flower blooms it smells of rotting flesh, to attract insects that usually like to feed on flesh and poo. It grows in the rainforests of Western Sumatra, Indonesia.

The **smallest** plant in the world is watermeal—it would take about 5,000 plants to fill one thimble! It floats on water, growing in lakes and streams and is eaten by birds.

The **oldest** plant we know of is in a fossil found in China. It is like a seaweed but about the size of a grain of rice and is 1 billion years old!

The **oldest living tree** is 4,853 years old! It lives somewhere in California—where it is exactly is kept a secret for its own safety. It has lived so long because it is adapted to live in harsh desert conditions.

The tree with the **thickest** trunk is called Árbol del Tule and it is in Oaxaca, Mexico. It is 137.8 feet around and 38 feet across.

Find the record-breakers in this plant shop.

Tallest
Smallest
Spikiest
Most petals
Longest leaves
The only plant with a red flower

Answers on page 32.

ANSWERS

page 5

page 7

page 9

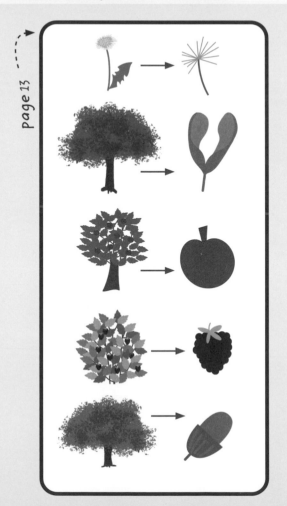

Page 13

page 15

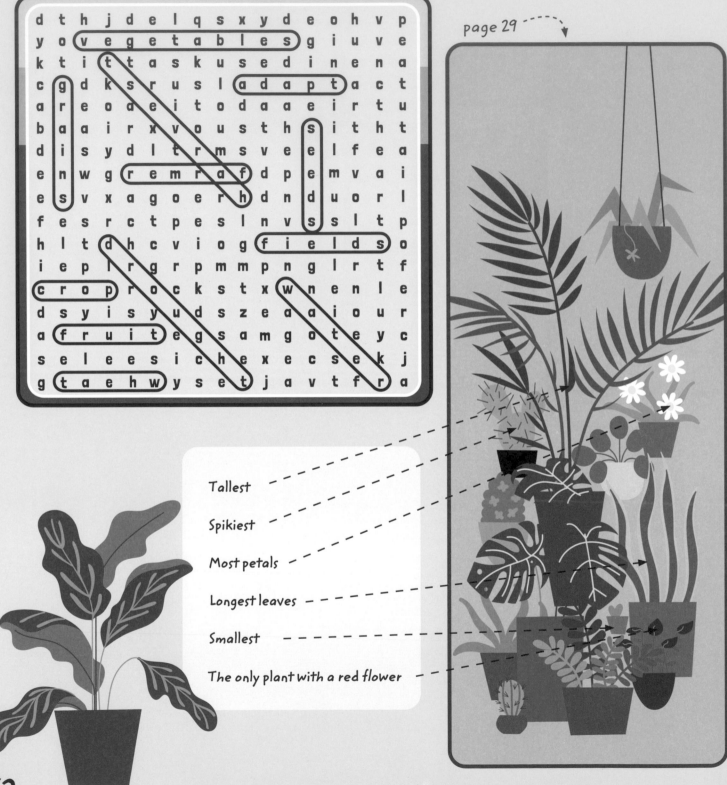

page 23

page 29

Tallest

Spikiest

Most petals

Longest leaves

Smallest

The only plant with a red flower